OLIVER HAD A FEELING

Words By: Cathryn Perry
Illustrations By: Latu Arifian

Published October 2019 by Wandering Roots Publishing

Copyright 2019 by Cathryn Perry
All rights reserved. No part of this publication may be reproduced or transmitted in any form or by any means electronic or mechanical, including photocopy recording, or any information storage and retrieval system, without permission in writing from the copyright owner.

ISBN: 978-1-951049-06-5

The sun in the sky brightly shone,
at the start of a beautiful day.
So, Oliver woke up and said,
"I want to go outside and play!"

Oliver had a bad feeling, because things were not going his way.

This feeling was angry and big, like he'd lost all the fun in his day.

The feeling grew bigger, and bigger. He looked at his mom and his dad.

He got red and turned hot in the face. He stomped and he said,

Then Oliver's Dad picks him up, and with Mom, hugs the boy really tight.
We are sorry you're mad about this, we will play with you outside tonight!

In the strong warm embrace of his parents
the feeling was melting away.
Oliver felt better soon,
and was ready to seize the new day!

The ride to the market was quick,
and Oliver learned a new song.

when Mom turned the radio up
and Daddy was singing along!

Oliver had a good feeling
because things were now going his way,

this feeling was joyful and fun
like he'd found something
good for today.

The feeling was tickling his tummy,
it felt very zippy and zappy.

Then Oliver grinned really big
and cheered from his heart,

The store was so busy and bright!
The people and music were loud!
Oliver wanted to leave,
to somewhere that's far from the crowd.

Dad said,
"Milk and fresh bread are on special,
what else do we need at the store?"
As Oliver asked for some candy,
like gummy bears, chocolate and more!

Oh no, little one, not today,
We are not getting candy Mom said.
"We'll put healthy foods in our basket,
like apples and peaches, and bread."

The feeling that Oliver had
was not good, it was heavy and bad,

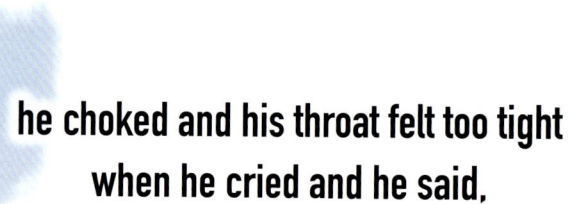

he choked and his throat felt too tight
when he cried and he said,

Dad stopped the cart in the middle and cuddled his sad little boy. "Thank you for telling your feelings, now help us in making some joy! "

Dad whispered a silly idea,
"We'll make it a challenge instead!
You can point out the foods on our list,
and I'll put them on top of my head!"

They laughed until dad dropped the eggs,
and the list,
a big melon,
and money.

But the family dog started barking, and knocked down a bag on the floor. Oliver wanted to sleep, but he wasn't asleep anymore!

The feeling that Oliver felt,
not getting the sleep he desired,

rubbing his eyes, feeling dizzy,

he yawned and he said,

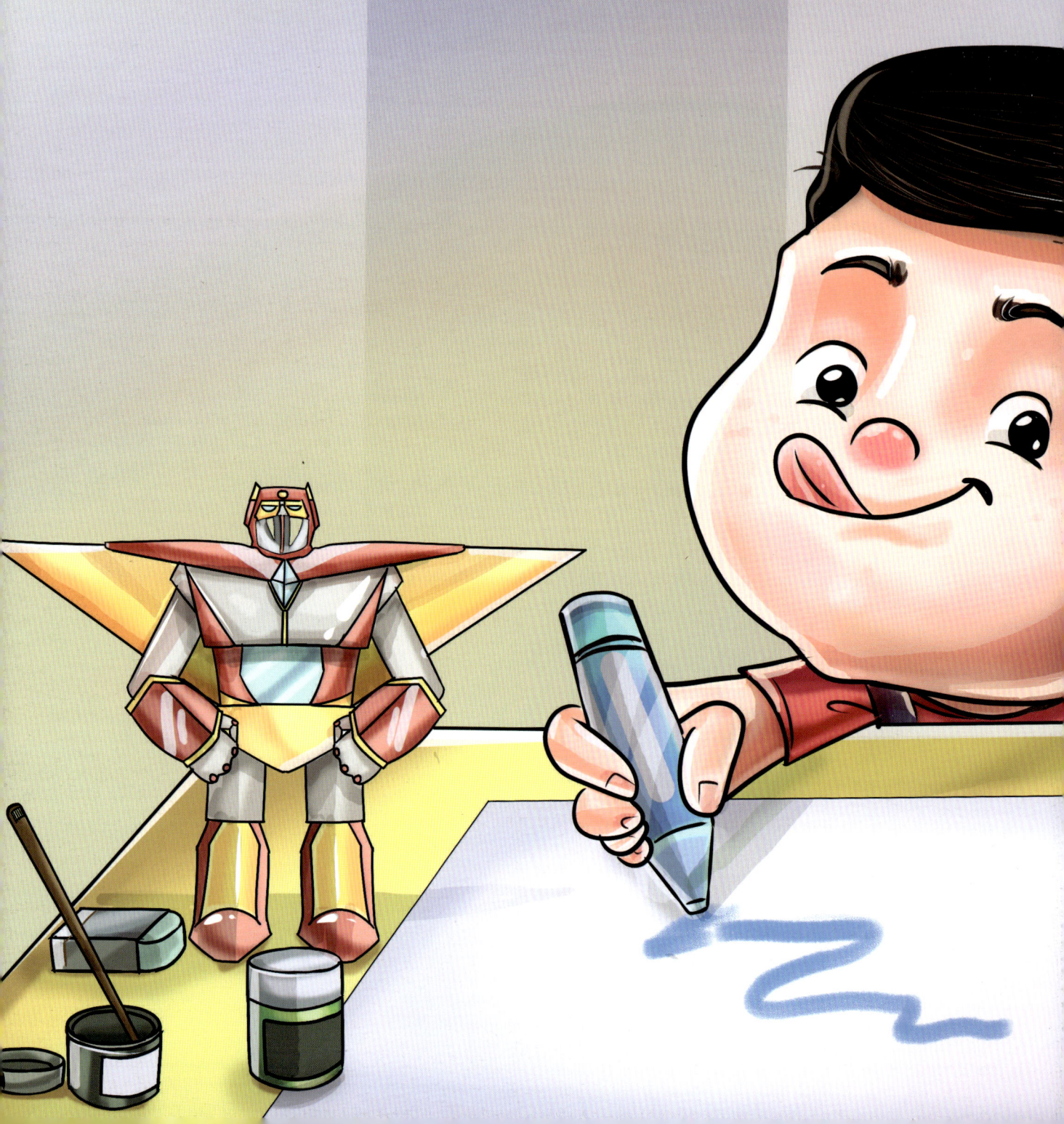

He felt proud of the gift he had made,
and off to his family, he flew!

His Mom and his Dad had big smiles
when they saw the nice card that he drew!

I'm HAPPY you read this book!